Virginia Hewitt

Beauty and the Banknote
Images of Women on Paper Money

Published for the
Trustees of the British Museum by
British Museum Press

For Fiona, true friendship personified...

The author, publisher, and Trustees of the British Museum gratefully acknowledge the support of Thomas De La Rue and Company Limited, Bemrose Security and Promotional Printing, and Portals Limited.

This book accompanies an exhibition of the same title, held in the British Museum from 17 May to 18 September 1994 to mark the 300th anniversary of the foundation of the Bank of England.

Notes and details of designs are not necessarily shown life-size. Actual dimensions for the whole note are given in millimetres at the end of each caption, width first. Dates refer to the first year of issue, the date given on the note, or the period during which the note was in circulation.

front cover: head of Britannia from a 5 pound note of the Bank of England, 1957.
back cover: allegorical woman from a 100 franc note of the Banque de France, 1915.
frontispiece: head of a woman from a 10 cedi note of the Bank of Ghana, 1982.

© 1994 Trustees of the British Museum

Second impression 1994

Published by British Museum Press
a division of British Museum Publications Limited
46 Bloomsbury Street
London WC1B 3QQ

British Library Cataloguing in Publication Data
A catalogue record for this book is
available from the British Library

ISBN 0-7141-0877-4

Designed by Andrew Shoolbred

Printed in Great Britain by Henry Ling, Dorset

Contents

NA
10

Preface

On its foundation in 1694, the Bank of England decorated its first notes with a small figure of Britannia. In so doing the Bank started a trend later taken up by others as the practice of banking spread, and for the last two hundred years images of women, from allegory to portrait, have been an enduring feature of banknote design across the world.

Drawing on the collections of the British Museum and the Chartered Institute of Bankers, this book explores the diversity, purpose and legacy of these images. It would be impossible, and not necessarily instructive, to cover every example of female symbolism on notes; inevitably there have been difficult decisions about what to leave out. My approach has been to look thematically at different ways in which women have been depicted on notes and how these images conform to the specific function of note design, yet may also influence our wider perception of women.

The help of many friends and colleagues has added to my pleasure in working on this project. Good illustrations are clearly vital, and I am indebted to Stephen Dodd for photographing all the notes with such care and attention, and to the designer, Andrew Shoolbred, for his sympathetic integration of text and pictures. The inclusion of colour plates was made possible by generous sponsorship from Thomas De La Rue and Company Limited, Bemrose Security and Promotional Printing, and Portals Limited, while the Bank of England kindly gave special permission regarding the reproduction of details from their notes and a British Treasury issue. Suzanne Haberfeld and Mirei Saito were responsible for the elegant cover design. My thanks also go to Joanna Champness and Julie Young for their advice on production.

I am immensely grateful for the interest and support of family, friends, and my colleagues in the Department of Coins and Medals – especially Philip Attwood, Andrew Burnett, Barrie Cook, Joe Cribb, Beverley Fryer, Kath Ireland, Janet Larkin, Elizabeth Savage, Cathy Sheffield and Luke Syson. Helen Wang provided both specific information on Far Eastern notes and much-appreciated general encouragement.

There remain three people whom I wish to thank above even these others. I have been helped tremendously by the enthusiasm and good sense of Nina Shandloff and Julia Walton, valued friends as well as editors. Finally, the commitment, skill and good humour of Margaret Massey, who typed and prepared the entire text in finished format for publication, defy yet again conventional words of praise.

1　A Woman's Work
The role of women on notes

A woman's work is never done.

Anon proverb

In December 1818 R.H. Solly, an English art critic, suggested that the Bank of England should introduce 'a beautiful female face' on their notes.[1] He was not being chauvinist or patronising: as an alternative he recommended 'one of the fine heads' – sex unspecified – 'in the British Museum, to which the public have free access'.[2] Solly's point was that circulating money should command the public's attention by carrying an image which everyone could recognise. No doubt he had in mind an idealised or classical form, but in proposing a human face he touched on a fundamental principle of perception. There is nothing we respond to so immediately as another of our own kind, and the human face, indeed usually that of a woman, is one of the first sights that as infants we see and know.

Human figures did in fact come into general use on banknotes during the nineteenth century, and more recently faces, often portraits, have become almost an integral part of banknote design worldwide. Certainly women have no monopoly in this market; men, children and animals are well-represented, as are less personal themes of landscape or architecture. But no other subject exhibits such variety and vitality as that of women on notes. From cool allegory to haughty beauty, they express far more than their creators may have intended or realised, revealing the growth of banking as a profession, political and national aspirations, and beyond this, underlying attitudes to women and the symbolic female form.

The women on notes have been chosen to play specific roles, however, for banknote designs are not the result of whim or accident. Today we use our own currency with scarcely a glance, but that is only possible because we are familiar enough with the notes to have confidence in them. In a foreign country with unfamiliar money, it is quite a different matter. The visual content of notes is therefore essential in enabling them to fulfil their function. Security against forgery is a major consideration, but the first, basic purpose of the design must be to show what the note is, who issued it, and how much it is worth. A banknote is in effect an advertisement – for a bank, a country, even for itself – and it is for this reason that human figures or faces are so effective, since they not only attract our attention, but also provoke an emotional response. If the first duty of a note's design is to declare its identity, the second is to engage the holder's confidence in its quality: the soundness of the currency, the stability of a bank, the greatness of a nation. That sounds straightforward enough, but in fact the interpretation of these qualities is inevitably subjective. The producer's choice of design and the consumer's reaction will be influenced by conscious objective assessment and by unconscious, personal attitudes, both of which must be considered if we are to understand the full message of women on notes.

For any issuing authority, be it a bank or central government, the message to be conveyed is one of security and viability. Unlike gold or silver, paper has no intrinsic value, so its use as money requires faith. That we trust paper money nowadays is in large part due to custom (we have no experience of relying on coins alone, and in any case, our coins are tokens, too, without precious metal content), but underlying that is an assumption that the source of the notes is reliable. 'As safe as the Bank of England', people say, in the ultimate accolade of trustworthiness. But the viability of a bank depends on several factors, the relative importance of which has changed over time. The first experiments with circulating paper money – in the tenth century AD in China and the seventeenth century in Europe and North America – were conducted under circumstances of considerable uncertainty: for example, merchants looking for ways to improve trade or colonies trying to compensate for lack of coin. Even when banks and the use of notes as circulating currency began to become widespread, in the eighteenth and nineteenth centuries, legislation to guarantee backing for the notes was at best inadequate, at worst, non-existent. At a time when the main qualification for being a banker was simply to declare yourself to be one, it was in the interests of good practitioners and bad to attract customers by declaring their integrity and solvency: the 'fortune, probity and prudence' defined by Adam Smith as essential to sound banking.[3] In the second half of the nineteenth century, laws to regulate banking practices reduced the risk of failure, and restricted the right of note issue to a smaller number of larger banks. Though still not guaranteed, financial viability could more readily be taken for granted, and newly professional banks emphasised instead their scale, status and authority. In the twentieth century, note issue has become almost exclusively the right of central banks and governments. Solvency is assumed; immense scale is self-evident; status is official. Banknotes are international ambassadors, and the images they carry represent not the banks, which are so institutionalised as to be devoid of personality, but countries and national identities.

1 Three demure nymphs on a 5 dollar note of the Allegany County Bank, Maryland, 1862. (186x77)

All these desirable characteristics – solvency, authority and nationality – have been embodied on notes by female figures. Wealth may be suggested by a classical allegory of Plenty; national prosperity by women harvesting an abundant crop. The explanation of this continuous starring role lies not just in the message of the banks, but also in the wider application of women as symbols, for however specific the purpose of banknote design, it has not for the most part generated a unique visual language or iconography, but has adapted existing conventions.[4] With the exception of female portraits, which are relatively rare and will be discussed in a later chapter, almost all women on notes are personifications or idealisations, even when they appear in a realistic form. In many societies idealised female images have been summoned to act as metaphors, in myth and dream, folklore and fine art. Such creatures have their origins in the conception that an elusive, mutable feminine principle governs emotion and intuition, creation through change, and personal relations, while a masculine principle rules reason, intellect and initiative. This assumption tends to result in individual named male heroes, and the use of female figures to personify abstract and universal concepts, such as justice, plenty or commerce.[5] At the same time, images of women may bring a particularly potent personal dimension to inanimate objects.

Drawing on the broad scope of this common ancestry, the women on banknotes have adopted different guises in different situations. One important factor has been

2 Figures on a German 20 Mark note of 1915 reflect the symbolic association of woman with the moon and intuition, man with daylight and reason. (140x90)

the growth of banking as a profession. All those offering professional skills face a dilemma, in that their success depends on attracting people by publicising their expertise, but the emphasis on their special abilities can have an alienating effect. Exclusivity and accessibility have somehow to be kept in play together, though circumstances may require emphasising one more than the other. This is one reason why early bankers, generally operating in a limited local area and known to their customers, might choose rather impersonal classical allegories of Justice or Industry to lend *gravitas* to their note issues. Later, large central banks still used personifications, but with more lifelike faces, suggesting both authority and personality. The trend towards friendly images has continued on twentieth-century notes, with increasingly realistic figures and portraits meeting our need for personal attention, while still representing the wider community.

It is worth remarking here that neither in intention nor effect have women on notes conferred on banking the stereotype of feminine weakness. Two rare instances of such a connection come from the most testing period of British banking history. The Bank of England's affectionate nickname 'The Old Lady of Threadneedle Street' first appeared in print in a cartoon drawn by James Gillray in 1797, personifying the Bank as a distressed elderly woman fighting off the grasping hands of the then Prime Minister, William Pitt. A quarter of a century later, during the commercial crisis of 1825-6, a newspaper article compared the reputation of a bank to a woman's honour, both liable to ruin at the merest hint of rumour.[6] These comparisons make their point by focusing on feminine frailty and vulnerability, but they do so only to underline the importance of integrity. Today the Bank of England's soubriquet indicates the respect due to one of the first great central banks, still in business after three hundred years and the demands of many prime ministers. It is such fundamentally 'good' qualities as enduring strength and trustworthiness which female figures have embodied on banknotes. In so doing, they have, however, bestowed their goodness not only upon the issuing bank or country, but also on the notes themselves.

Theoretically, money may be seen simply as a convenient tool facilitating the distribution and exchange of goods and services; in reality, while money itself is neutral, the people who handle it are not. Both in use and as a concept, money arouses complex feelings, which are not necessarily all positive. From biblical times we have been taught that man cannot serve God and Mammon, that the love of money leads to evil. Obviously this does not mean that money in itself is bad, but it does point up an unease, and uncertainty as to what attitude we should properly take. People are often reluctant to admit, even to themselves, how much they care about money, but negotiating its use and distribution can reveal strong feelings and cause deep disagreement. Not for nothing is money considered a taboo topic in polite conversation. Good images alone on notes will not be enough to exorcise any negative connotations, but inappropriate ones will almost certainly aggravate them. Evidence of such an instinctive reaction is most easily found in those societies which openly incorporate the role of myth and intuition in everyday life: for example, the unwillingness of the Wahgi peoples in Papua New Guinea to keep banknotes with designs which they believed represented the spirits of the money's ancestral owners.[7] If this seems far removed from our idea of 'rational' culture, it should be remembered how often we attach emotional or superstitious value to money: coins for luck in a Christmas pudding; gifts left by the Tooth Fairy; banknotes inscribed with loving wishes and sent by soldiers abroad to their sweethearts at home. These rituals take no account of the designs on coins and notes, but they are a reminder that our own attitudes to money are not dictated simply by practical need.

Our emotional response to money is therefore another reason for images on notes to have positive associations; thus political upheaval is commemorated on notes by scenes of joy at the new order – for example, Filipino soldiers, raising guns in nationalist triumph in 1898 or crowds cheering the Ayatollah in Iran in 1981 – and not the anger and violence through which change occurred. Here it is important to appreciate that what is well-regarded in one society may be condemned in another: smoking factory chimneys may signal economic growth in an industrialising nation; to post-industrial western Europe they reek of pollution. The same considerations

3 *left* Guanyin, goddess of mercy, on a Chinese 'Hell note'
(reproduction money for ritual burning at funerals), 1980s. (168x94)
4 *right* Cheerfully burdened woman on a 1000 franc note of Tahiti, 1940s-50s. (209x120)

apply to the presentation of women; if they are to impart moral rectitude to notes, they must comply with the expectations of their culture. This may be achieved quite innocently, with a face or hairstyle clearly belonging to a particular era; or it may involve more complex implications, as with native girls smiling under beneficent colonial rule, or healthy workers contributing to the communist state. While there is an underlying common thread of 'goodness', and certain chronological and geographical patterns may be discerned, the varied female forms on notes defy rigid definition, following instead the vagaries of human history. Once again, it is the capacity to adapt which equips the feminine as metaphor and messenger.

Of course we use paper money every day without any regard for these deeper layers of meaning. Trusting in the long tradition of banking and pressed by the urgent pace of modern living, we take banknotes completely for granted. Yet it is their very success which makes the images they carry so important. Notes are among the most mass-produced objects in the world, painstakingly designed for millions of people to use. They offer an unparalleled opportunity for officially-sanctioned propaganda, to colour the recipient's views. But their creators are no less subject to influence and suggestion, and they cannot always predict how their message will be received. It is at this conjunction of conscious choice and unconscious response that female images on notes exercise their hidden power, reflecting and reinforcing our conflicting perceptions of women and their place in society.

5 Allegory with telephone and skyscrapers on a 1000 dollar note of Ecuador, 1940s-60s. (188x90)

2 Beauty and Virtue
Woman as allegory

In a sense all women on banknotes, even portraits, are allegorical in that they symbolise something beyond themselves. Nevertheless there is a distinction between lifelike portrayals of women in realistic situations, however idealised, and those clearly imaginary beings who give human, female form to abstract concepts and qualities. These virtuous personifications were at the height of their power in the nineteenth century, but have continued to bestow their blessings on modern notes.

In the western world, from the late eighteenth to at least the mid-nineteenth century, allegorical figures emerged from a harmonious union of artistic, commercial and philosophical endeavour, in which society strove for moral worth by looking back to the perceived nobility and grace of the classical world. Both political and industrial revolutions, though paid for by exploited labour, and fostering opportunism and greed, were still fired by high ideals for the common good, and it is the desired end, not the painful means, which is represented in the contemporary symbolism on banknotes: triumphant Liberty, fair-minded Justice, and generous Plenty with fruits of the earth for all to share. The issue and circulation of paper money became widespread under just such turbulent circumstances, but in order to be trusted, the money itself had to suggest not struggle, but stability. So on the paper money of revolutionary France (fig. 7) and the local banknotes of industrialising Britain in the 1810s and 1820s, graceful female personifications offered reassurance as to the political and commercial health of their nations.

Over time, the significance of those images has widened to include not only the ideals which they represent, but also their particular role on paper money. Prior to the late eighteenth century, paper currency had little pictorial content, consisting predominantly of written text with perhaps some simple ornament. Engravings of female allegories, drawing on the fashion for neo-classical forms, were among the first representational images to be widely used on banknotes. Inevitably the design of notes has evolved in line with changes in banking, aesthetic taste, and printing technology, but the process has been gradual. New designs on objects for mass consumption do not arrive unheralded or unbidden, and on such official documents as banknotes, existing traditions are a major influence on innovation. Furthermore,

6 Allegory with tools and fruits of agriculture on a 1 dollar note of Canada, 1935. (150x72)

7 *left* Symbols of fortune, victory and freedom on a French note for 50 livres, 1792. (186x111)
8 Justice with her sword and scales on a 2 dollar note of the Baltimore Savings Institution, 1840. (180x79)

the good qualities embodied by female allegories remain fundamental to sound currency. From a historical viewpoint, therefore, these beings can be seen as prototypes for future generations of women on notes.

At first sight allegorical women on notes may appear merely decorative and rather insubstantial; closer inspection shows them to be multi-faceted, reflecting the complexity of the banks' message, and the ambiguity of the feminine character. The success of any monetary authority will depend on security, and it is not surprising that many female allegories impart a sense of power and authority. Figures of Britannia, Justice, and Law all represent conditions of strength and autonomy necessary for the maintenance and control of wealth. Though clearly female, they are seldom womanly, subjugating personality to the superhuman demands of their role. Personifications of countries are often heavily armoured with helmet and breastplate, boasting an almost masculine aggression, while, Justice, even when carrying a sword, usually has an air of calm detachment, poised loftily above the petty dealings of humanity. These are women made chaste, guarding a nation's wealth not with feminine charms, but by their very impregnability.

The cold, impersonal exterior of such élite beings is, however, often qualified by tell-tale signs of life in their attributes and facial expressions. The frequent presence of an animal, usually a lion, is of particular interest here. As the king of beasts, symbol of courage, majesty and guardianship, the lion is a natural companion for patriotic figures of, say, Britannia, or Svea in Sweden, and this, no doubt, is the association intended by those choosing the image. But the lion is also fierce and wild – indeed, this is the source of its power – and may also suggest the untamed, uncontrollable aspect of woman. In the mythology of ancient civilisations, goddesses were frequently depicted as animals, and ferocious ones at that – lions, boars and bears, while many cultures have unconsciously equated women with the dangerous 'other',[8] that is, the non-human or animal. Female allegories accompanied by lions therefore deliver an ambiguous message of inviolate, almost asexual authority, which nonetheless draws its power from inherent wildness. A striking example is found on an early twentieth-century note from Brazil: a bored, helmeted maiden, idly holding a thick oak branch and surrounded by heavy books of law, reclines against a sleeping lion, her left hand dangling in its fur. Both lion and woman are relaxed, at rest, but it would be folly to disturb them (fig. 10).

Power alone, however, cannot create wealth, and sterile figures of authority are balanced by fertile images of abundance. Graceful allegories with ships, tools and fruit appear frequently to personify trade, industry and agriculture, the means of production which generate economic activity and the wealth of nations. Sometimes the references are quite specific: in the nineteenth century, the livelihood of many banks depended on local business, which was acknowledged on their notes; for instance, grazing cattle and wheatfields feature prominently on the notes of America and Canada. But in a broader sense, too, commerce, agriculture and industry may all be used to suggest prosperity achieved through a process of growth and development. Both literally and metaphorically, such associations are appropriate for an institution issuing money; they are also particularly conducive to symbolism in female form. This is especially true of agriculture, for increase in wealth is equated with the nurture and harvesting of crops, which in turn parallels the woman's reproductive role. In this guise, female allegories on notes are often endowed with baskets of fresh produce, or a cornucopia (horn of plenty) overflowing with ripe fruit and vegetables.[9] Others indicate more explicitly their kinship with Ceres, goddess of agriculture, and are seen holding or protecting sheaves of corn, to signify new life, fertility and abundance. These women almost always carry a scythe, which serves both as a practical tool and as a symbol of the harvest, with its connotations of death followed by rebirth. Such imagery succinctly correlates the continuing fluctuations in economic wealth, the seasons in nature, and a woman's reproductive cycle. Indeed the intimation of continuity and renewal is

9 The mythological association of women with animals is illustrated on this 100 franc note of Tahiti, 1920, showing an allegorical figure and a native woman relaxing with a bull and tiger. (208x120)

10 The lion and the oak symbolise the power of Law on a 10 mil reis note of Brazil, 1907. (167x71)

11 *left* Female allegory with symbols of agriculture and trade on a 10 pound note
of the Bank of New South Wales, Melbourne, *c.*1850-60. (196x118)
12 Woman with corn and scythe on a 2 dollar note of the Bank of Washtenaw, Michigan, 1854. (185x72)

vital, since a successful bank will not only preserve capital, but use it to create more. The mysterious regenerative capacity of woman is perhaps most movingly shown on a Swiss note design in which aged women enter a fountain of youth to emerge restored to youth and beauty, while their barren staff is transformed into an exquisite rose (fig. 13). Issued from the 1950s to the 1970s, this is an unusually modern example of such enigmatic allegory.

Allegorical women on notes may appear as either protectors or progenitors of wealth, but these roles are not mutually exclusive. Political and military strength are conducive to creating and amassing wealth, but the possession of wealth is in itself an effective form of authority. Some banknotes illustrate both functions, either by combining two or more figures – say, Britannia with Plenty – or by endowing one multi-talented creature with an array of attributes for power and production. Where several figures appear, their composition will convey varying chains of command. Thus a note from mid-nineteenth-century Canada carries one vignette of Britannia and Justice, walking side by side on equal terms, and another with a seated figure of Plenty, gazing gratefully up at a standing Britannia who brandishes spear and

13 Age turns to youth, winter to spring on a design entitled 'Fountain of Youth'
on a Swiss 500 franc note, 1957-73. (209x114)

14 Britannia with Justice (*left*) and Plenty (*right*) on a 5 dollar note
of The Farmer's Joint Stock Bank, Toronto, 1849. (180x78)

15 Germania upheld by industry and agriculture on a German 100 Mark note, 1908. (158x101)

shield (fig. 14). In contrast, a German note of the early twentieth century shows two strapping personifications of agriculture and industry supporting the framed head of Germania (fig. 15). Seen in their official context, these allegories represent characteristics which are desirable for a money-issuing authority; self-effacing, they allow the viewer to project on to them a universal symbolism. Yet they are not completely devoid of personality, and the values they uphold have a far-reaching application, embodying in female form the perceived duality of woman's nature, which may employ strength in the cause of life and peace.

Britannia and her sisters
Perhaps the most familiar female allegories on banknotes are the stately representatives of nationhood. The Bank of England chose Britannia for its seal at its foundation in 1694, and she has since appeared on every note the Bank has issued. Such a supreme being cannot be monopolised, however, and Britannia has also lent her weight to many private, provincial issues, sometimes joining forces with her kinswomen Hibernia and Scotia (fig. 16), who may also be found independently on the notes of Ireland and Scotland. Generally, though, personifications of a state are associated with issues of central banks, and they appear splendidly arrayed to reflect the glory of their nation.

It has been suggested that these figures of nationhood trace their ancestry back to Athena, goddess of war,[10] and it is true that many are grimly armed with helmet and breastplate, sword and shield. A few even wear Athena's medusa-head brooch, either on breastplate or helmet. In some cases the gorgon is replaced by an equally terrifying lion's head (fig. 17); often the entire animal rests watchfully by the woman's side. Despite their battery of arms, it is, however, uncommon for national personifications to be explicitly warlike: a possible exception is the intimidating standing Britannia introduced on British Treasury notes in 1918 (fig. 18). For the most part they are protective figures of authority, often seated, and surrounded by symbols of their realm, such as hammers and ploughshares or cornucopiae spilling out coins. An elegant figure of Russia holds in one hand a glittering sceptre, in the other a branch of evergreen laurel, signifying victory (fig. 19); Germania guards the wheels of industry, the crops of agriculture, and a child holding a dove of peace (fig. 20). Athena, in ancient times, was also the protector of home and family, and here aggression is harnessed in the service of peace, might for right – at least in the eyes of those issuing the notes. Superior Britannias on the nineteenth-century notes of Canada can be seen as early examples of paternalist colonialism which may not have been so attractive to those on the receiving end. There is then a certain tension in these allegories, which may affect our response to them as images of women. Encased in hard masculine armour, they may seem to be de-sexed, women absorbed into a male culture, but at the same time, the very inversion of a traditional female image may simply emphasise the grip of that convention.[11] The same conundrum is posed by personifications of power that are presented in an

16 Britannia, Hibernia and Scotia on a 1 pound note for the Ringwood and Poole Bank, 1820s. (191x96)

17 *left* Britannia with breastplate, spear and lion on helmet on a 25 cent note of Canada, 1870. (111x56)
18 *right* Proud Britannia on British Treasury 10 shilling note of 1918 to 1927. (136x77)

19 Russia bedecked and bejewelled on a 500 rouble note of 1912 to 1917. (273x126)

20 Germania with symbols of peace, trade, agriculture and industry on a 5 Mark note of 1904. (125x80)

21 Glamorous Svea with lion and coins on a commemorative 10 kronor note of Sweden, 1968. (120x68)

unashamedly 'feminine' light, for despite their regal trappings, they often do not conform to our stereotyped idea of authority. Sweden provides a case in point; in 1968 the Sveriges Riksbank issued a commemorative note for its tercentenary, depicting a new version of the seated figure of Svea who had long been featured on its notes. Although she retains her classical attributes, she is a child of her time: her pose is languid, one elbow resting casually on the cornucopia of coins; her contemporary face turns coyly away; a slender neck accentuates her swelling breasts. She is a queen, indeed, but of catwalk or cinema screen, not a country (fig. 21).

Liberty and Law
Freedom is an important corollary of state power, for political independence may be regarded as a prerequisite for a true sense of national identity. Such liberty is victory's prize, but if the benefits are to be upheld, a system of law and justice must be imposed. The qualities of victory, liberty and justice have all been symbolised on notes by female allegories who, like their patriotic cousins considered above, impart an image of authority. As befits their stirring, emotional call, figures suggesting Liberty or Victory are often dynamic, moving confidently forward. Two notes from France and Greece reproduce great artistic interpretations of Liberty and Victory: the Banque de France 100 franc note introduced in 1978 accompanies a portrait of Eugène Delacroix with a detail from his painting of 'Liberty leading the People' (fig. 22), while on a note of 1942 Greece displays the glorious Winged Victory of Samothrace (fig. 23). Ostensibly, both combine political statement with cultural heritage, but the balance is different in each case: for Delacroix's 'Liberty', rendered in an inappropriately sketchy hand, the official nature of the new medium seems to dilute her message; but Greece's ancient Victory, called forth in the middle of World War II and presiding over town and country, moves towards the viewer with an insistent power that challenges the confines of her narrow paper context.

Personifications of Justice and Law are, predictably, more constrained and constraining. An ornate Austrian note of 1866 juxtaposes a militant male warrior and lion with a stern female figure pointing to a book of Law; at her feet is a resentful dragon with firmly manacled claws (fig. 24). This civilising aspect of authority may also be seen on colonial note issues, where the role of liberty is decidedly double-edged. A note of Algeria in the 1940s shows a naked native boy offering fruit to a seated female figure (fig. 25). She is clothed, and protected by breastplate and sword; she rests one hand on the boy's shoulder, while the other points to an open book. An exchange is taking place, food for learning, but there is no doubt about who is in control: this mother country has a distinctly chauvinist air.

Yet not all these figures are so formidable. Some are content to play a quieter part, especially when they share the stage with a wider range of symbols. American private bank issues of the nineteenth century often carry vignettes of demure girls

22 Delacroix and 'Liberty leading the People' on a 100 franc note of France, 1978 to present. (159x84)

23 Winged Victory of Samothrace on a 5000 drachmae note of the Bank of Greece, 1942. (166x83)

24 The authority of Law (*right*) on an Austrian 50 gulden note, 1866. (196x131)

25 Colonial gifts handed to a personified western mother country, who wears
a breastplate with gorgon's head. Algeria, 500 francs, 1944. (200x122)

26 Allegory with eagle, shield and cap of liberty on a 1 dollar note
of the Bank of Augusta, Georgia, 1840s-50s. (183x83)

27 Playful allegories surrounded by symbols of authority on a 50 mil reis note of Brazil, 1916. (182x87)

sitting relaxed among stars and stripes and piles of coins. Sometimes, caps of liberty and swords of justice may appear to give the lie to their gentle demeanour, but even here alighting eagles symbolically equate state power with spiritual victory (fig. 26). Once again, Brazil offers a most appealing if ambiguous image: two seated allegories are swamped with potent accoutrements, swords and fasces, scrolls and corn-ears. But these are turned to toys by the playful expressions of the women, who wear their glamorous breastplates and bushy laurel wreaths as though they were costumes for dressing-up (fig. 27).

Wealth in abundance

Free from the constraints of power, female allegories representing fertility, growth and trade are amongst the most serene and invitingly feminine. Swords are replaced by ploughshares, and armour discarded in favour of soft draperies, frequently parted to expose one breast. There is an obvious analogy between agricultural and industrial growth, distributed by trade to feed the nation, and woman's reproductive, nurturing role, and it is perhaps because of this that the female images associated with agriculture often have the sweetest faces and most shapely figures. Surprisingly, there are relatively few banknotes making direct comparison between motherhood and prosperity. An attractive exception from Martinique shows a healthy baby playing beside a young woman with windswept cloak and hair, full of energy and movement (fig. 28). They are nourished by a basket heaped with plump bunches of grapes, symbols of the wine of life and immortality. Here the imagery is classically allusive; a more explicit example comes from a Swiss note design entitled 'Apple Harvest', in which round, ripe apples are a graphic echo of the full breast of a mother suckling her child (fig. 29).

28 A woman and child with ripe grapes symbolise life on a 100 franc note of Martinique, 1942. (178x87)

29 'Apple Harvest' design, symbolising fertility, on a Swiss 50 franc note, 1955-74. (174x95)

30 Male Labour and female Prosperity on a Dutch 10 gulden note, 1921. (168x97)

More often, and especially on nineteenth-century notes, the connection between economic growth and female fertility is entirely implicit, a sub-text conveyed by the combination of female figures with life-giving attributes: sheaves of corn, sacks of grain, buzzing beehives, and cornucopiae of fruit or coins. The attributes may even include machinery, for although the images sometimes reflect a sexual division of labour allocating men to heavy industrial work and women to reaping agricultural produce, generally a female allegory is present to oversee the whole process. As so often, the message is mixed. It may be automatic now to condemn such stereotyped roles as patronising, but these men have no evident superiority. Often, in fact, it is the women who appear dominant; for instance in 1921 a contemporary Dutch note was satirised for allowing a shirtless, barefoot blacksmith to address an elegant, well-bred Prosperity (fig. 30).[12]

However, even lone women calmly surveying city, land and sea give little impression of real female power. In practice women have seldom exercised visible economic control, contributing rather as part of the workforce themselves, or indirectly by bearing children who will become workers. As with the armour-plated guardians of the state, so the wealth-giving power of these imaginary beings may only serve to point up the muted status of real women.

31 Allegory representing trade and commerce on a 100 escudo note
of the Cape Verde Islands, 1958. (160x84)

3 Beauty's Self
A woman's body

My love in her attire doth show her wit
It doth so well become her;
For every season she hath dressings fit,
For Winter, Spring and Summer
No beauty she doth miss
When all her robes are on:
But Beauty's self she is
When all her robes are gone.

Anon (from A Poetical Rhapsody, 1602)

During the course of the twentieth century, the depiction of imaginary female personifications on banknotes has given way to naturalistic images of women in scenes of everyday life. The women thus portrayed still play an important symbolic role, but are more likely to be defined by the tasks they are performing. The realism of the designs tends to obscure their symbolic meaning, and this affects our reaction to them as images of women.

The different functions of allegorical and lifelike women are vividly illustrated on a note of French West Africa of the 1940s, which shows a young native woman with her baby next to a female allegory who represents France (pl. 3). The allegory rests one hand protectively on the woman's shoulder, while the other is clasped by the baby, their pale and dark fingers intertwined. In the background are two fainter images, a clothed allegory behind the mother joining hands with a naked native woman behind the foreground allegory. With its striking contrasts of fantasy and reality, white and black, dress and undress, the image combines several aspects of the role of women on notes, such as the authority of the allegory, the domesticity of the African woman and the ambiguous allure of the female nude.

The change from allegory to realism is to a large extent bound up with the shift in responsibility for note issue from small local banks to large-scale central institutions, which has stimulated new methods of note production to meet increasing demand, and the resulting need for greater protection against forgery. Advances in printing technology have encouraged the introduction of complex colour printing and expansion of the pictorial element to cover both front and back of the note, dominating the written text. This certainly offers greater scope for attractively composed naturalistic scenes, but should be seen as facilitating rather than causing changes in the content of note design; vignettes of realistic scenes were sometimes used on nineteenth-century notes, and allegorical figures still appear on modern issues. Furthermore, although the continual search for more sophisticated printing has made banknote design a highly-specialised field of graphic art, radical change is generally restricted to technical innovation. The official nature of currency encourages conservatism in design, and new departures tend to grow out of established precedent. Consequently even the most up-to-date images may contain traditional symbols.

The switch from local notes to state-controlled national issues has probably been a more important influence for change in that the need to publicise the solvency of a bank has been superseded by the desire to express a distinctive cultural identity. Universal symbols of abstract qualities are therefore less pertinent than specific national emblems, and although these are invariably presented in a positive light, the choice of images will depend on the way a society defines good qualities. In Victorian Britain the importance of moral values in business transactions was openly recognised and appropriately represented by classical allegory, but modern society

32,33 Women carrying crops on their heads from (*left*) a 4 dollar note of the spurious Commercial Bank of Fort Erie, Upper Canada, 1837, and (*right*) a 20 mil reis note of Brazil, 1892. (183x78; 194x86)

has tended to separate spiritual and secular aspects of life, with the former increasingly regarded as a personal concern. Visual imagery for mass-consumption has become correspondingly realistic, sharply-focused and instantly accessible – except where it has degenerated into geometric logos so vague as to have virtually no meaning at all.[13] There is little place in public life today for high-minded Virtues, and it is not surprising that the incidence of classical personifications has declined on banknotes as in other spheres of art and architecture.

The changing content of note designs may also be attributed to the development of banking in non-western countries. Classical allegories are of European stock, and while they have been exported for use on overseas issues, particularly in the Americas and Australasia, they have limited meaning in other countries. A curious exception is the 'Chinese Britannia' on a note of the China and South Sea Bank (Chap. 4, fig. 65), though in fact both China and Japan, countries with a long tradition of issuing paper money, depict their own deities in human form on their notes. However, in the second half of the twentieth century, they too have given way to more realistic images of people and places. In Oceania, India and the Middle East, note designs tend to concentrate on traditional, non-figurative patterns or naturalistic scenes, and spiritual values are represented by pictures of, say, monuments or carvings (some of women) with religious or mythological significance (fig. 34).

Many kinds of image can be used to conjure up the spirit of a country, and landscape, architecture, folklore and history all offer rich material for note designs. Human figures have proved to be enduringly popular, however, either on their own or combined with other subjects. Three reasons may be suggested for this. One is that by bringing a personal dimension to the design, images of people attract our attention and speed up our recognition of a note, making it easier to use and harder to counterfeit successfully. Secondly, although classical virtues have gone out of fashion, state authorities still want to declare their good character, and character of any sort is more readily ascribed to a person than to an object. Finally, national identity is most fundamentally expressed by the people of a country and the societies they create. So images of women continue to proliferate on notes, though now they feature in more down-to-earth roles than the other-worldly allegories of former times.

Just as allegories may be described as symbols which have borrowed human form, so 'real' women on notes play a symbolic role, and certain aspects of their portrayal may continue or adapt earlier conventions. This is perhaps most apparent in scenes of women working in agriculture or industry, for these basic allusions to the means of economic growth and national wealth are perennially relevant as images on money. Usually the allegorical attributes of symbolic corn-ears, tools and wheels are transformed into whole fields and factories, but in many cultures fruits and plants still appear as indirect references to woman's fertility. A Czechoslovakian note design introduced in 1961 gives these traditional emblems a modern twist: a labourer

34 *top* The strong association of woman with the waters of life is symbolised by this famous
Syrian statue of a water goddess. Detail from a 50 pound note, Syria. (155x75)
35 *above* Woman associated with agricultural fertility and man with industry
on a 100 korun note of Czechoslovakia, 1961. (164x80)

stands next to a farm-girl, her arms full of corn; their heads are framed by a circle
composed of a stylised cog-wheel and ear of corn (fig. 35). To their right, in the
distance, is a bleak landscape of smoking industrial chimneys. This unlikely
combination of bucolic optimism and grimy reality stayed in circulation until 1993,
even continuing on the transitional currency of the new separate Slovak Republic,
remarkable evidence of the tendency to conservatism inherent in note design.

Despite the continued use of traditional symbols, naturalistic images of women on
notes do not create the same impression as allegorical figures. To some extent they
are not intended to, since, as we have seen, the money-issuing institutions they
represent have changed their nature and therefore the emphasis of their advertising.

But changing the medium has also, unwittingly, altered the message, in that the more realistic the scene, the less we need to look for deeper layers of meaning. We see women working in a paddy field, not the backbone of an economy, and this has implications for the way in which those notes affect our perception of women. It might seem that lifelike portrayals should have more positive impact, because we can more easily identify with pictures of women as individuals carrying out real tasks. The problem is that what they have gained in substance, they have lost in authority. A striking feature of allegories is that they seldom *do* very much: even when they are holding huge sheaves of corn or heavy swords, they do not seem to be expending any effort; they simply have an air of being in charge. Quite the opposite is true of women depicted naturalistically. They are shown as workers, not managers; nurses, not doctors; mothers of babies, not Mother Earth sustaining the whole of human existence. A similar contrast is revealed in the different connotations of nudity between allegorical and realistic women, for although some underlying meanings are shared, the natural bodies of the realistically-portrayed women lack the symbolic quality of nymphs in floating draperies. It is of course true that many of the scenes of women engaged in everyday tasks at home or at work are believable. It is also true that equating the domestic and professional lives of women with the creation of wealth does reflect the very real contribution women make in these areas. But this is oblique symbolism drawing on what is often an invisible and unacknowledged power, and it is disconcerting that autonomous female authority is more openly displayed in the form of imaginary beings. This is all the more disturbing because central banks and state treasuries invariably choose uncontroversial images for their currencies, and the process becomes self-fulfilling when the official nature of the notes seems to guarantee the authenticity of the images they carry. Thus the idea that women lack status and authority may be reinforced by naturalistic portrayals whose apparent meaning is sufficiently clear that we are not invited to look below the surface.

'A woman's place'
There are relatively few notes which show women in the home; perhaps such an informal and private context does not comply with the grand canvas covered by state authority. Women are, however, often seen employed in what are traditionally regarded as female domestic activities. Images of mother and child are most likely to suggest an enduring symbolic meaning, but even here, the focus seems to be on a mother's duty in child-rearing, rather than on woman as source of universal life. Charming nineteenth-century vignettes, such as those on North American issues showing loyal women providing refreshment for their hard-working menfolk (fig. 37), may well give an accurate, if romantic, view of women's role in creating solid foundations for a local community, and by inference, for its bank. A century later, women cannot convincingly be shown in such restricted roles, but domestic harmony is still something to prize. Two note designs from Switzerland and Brazil, issued

行
伍拾圓
50

2 *above* A woman in national costume, with attributes of agriculture and fertility, balances the male allegorical figure of Mercury with symbols of trade, on a 50 złotych note of Poland, 1929. (180 × 99)

3 *below* The contrasts of black and white, reality and fantasy are shown in symbolic unity on a 1000 franc note of French West Africa, *c*.1945. (195 × 110)

1 *previous page* On a 50 dollar note of the Hongkong and Shanghai Banking Corporation, 1930, an allegorical woman represents the bank's Chinese name, 'Abundant Exchange', with trays of fruits and the winged wheel of communications. (187 × 112)

4 *above* A barefoot woman raking branches on an unusually simple illustration for a 20 korun note of Czechoslovakia, 1949. (127 × 60)

5 *above* African women stamping maize against a background of traditional huts and cultivated fields on a 5 dollar note of Zimbabwe, 1983. (140 × 73)

6 Women picking cotton and working in a textile factory, major sources of economic wealth, on a 5000 franc note of Mali, 1971–3. (156 × 101)

7 *above left* Women working in cotton fields on a 50 pound note of Syria, 1958. Cotton is one of the country's major exports. (155 × 74)

8 *above right* Woman with short hair, wearing overalls, driving a tractor on a 1 yuan note of the People's Bank of China, 1960. (130 × 57)

9 *below* Young women and girls performing a traditional folk dance on a 1 lilangeni note of Swaziland, 1974. (150 × 68)

10 *above* A bare-breasted woman holding fruits and vegetables symbolises nourishment and fertility on a 100 franc note of French West Africa, 1948. (front of fig. 57; 162 × 90)

11 Native women and children in the marketplace represent national life and prosperity on a 1000 franc note of New Caledonia, a French colony in the South Pacific, *c*.1938–41. (210 × 119)

12 *above* Traditional costume and jewellery worn by a beautiful native woman on a 100 franc note of French West Africa, 1956–7. (128 × 83)

13 *above* A contemporary face with classical helmet and laurel on a 5 franc note of France, 1918. (124 × 80)

14 The turreted crown of Tyche, goddess of fortune, adorns this imperious allegory on a 10 peseta note of Republican Spain, 1935. (110 × 77)

15 The traditional symbol of laurel combined with glamorous make-up and modern hairstyles on a 1000 franc (later 20 new franc) note of Réunion, 1940s–60s. (185 × 100)

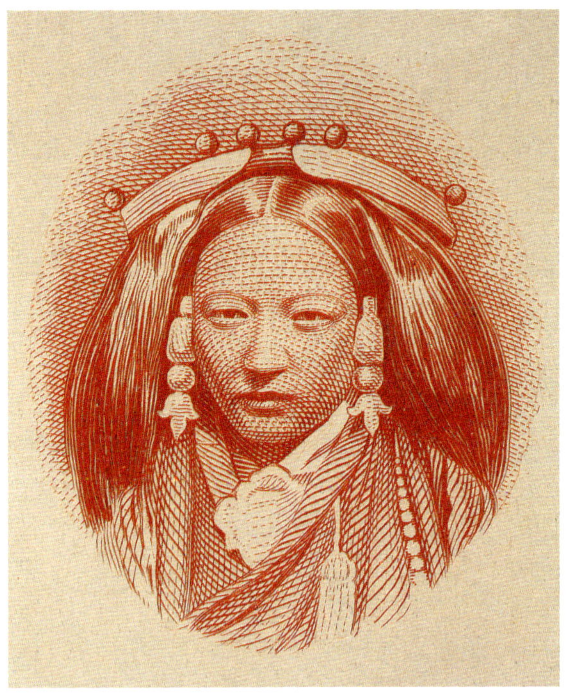

16 *above* Specimen colour printing of the head of a Tibetan woman wearing a native headdress, used on a 10 yuan note of the China and South Sea Bank Ltd, 1927. (178 × 89)

17 *above* Isabel, Queen of Portugal (1271–1336), canonised in 1626 for her life of prayer and good works, on a note for 50 escudos ouro, Portugal, 1964. (142 × 70)

18 The writer Selma Lagerlöf (1858–1940), who won the Nobel prize for literature in 1909, is the first woman represented on Swedish notes. Detail from a 20 kronor note, 1992. (130 × 71)

19 Portrait of Cecilia Meireles (1901–64), Brazilian writer and poet, which first appeared on the 100 new cruzado note of Brazil issued in 1989, the 25th anniversary of her death. (140 × 64)

20 Sumptuous plenty represented by a young girl garlanded with roses, her hands heaped with fruits, on a 50 Mark note of Germany, 1920. (150 × 99)

36 *above left* Regeneration symbolised by a mother and child with corn and scythe, on a 5 dong note of Vietnam, 1946. (66x129)
37 *above right* Woman providing male farm worker with refreshment on a 10 dollar note of the Bank of the Republic, Providence, Rhode Island. (177x77)
38 *below left* Domestic harmony on a Swiss 500 franc note of 1923. (199x127)

39 *above* Patriotic family scene for the centenary of the Republic on a 200 new cruzado note of Brazil, 1989. (138x63)

almost seventy years apart, try to resolve the problem by illustrating women in period costume peacefully sewing at home (figs. 38,39). The Brazilian scene is especially idealistic in that it is a detail from a painting in which a mother and family sewing the Republican flag are intended to symbolise national unity and freedom.[14]

While not denying the importance of domestic life, it must be said that the women shown in this context on notes conform to a stereotype, which is given spurious validation by their generally contented expressions. (Two tired, cross-looking women cooking something in a pot on a Brazilian note are a refreshing antidote (fig. 40)). Men are not shown in domestic situations except occasionally as fathers, who are figures of authority. The lines of sexual discrimination are pointedly drawn on Chinese private issues of the late nineteenth century, showing tiny vignettes of women in traditional scenes, surrounded by philosophical tracts on goodness, written by men (fig. 42). The Cinderella complex is captured perfectly on a Czechoslovakian note of the late 1940s (pl. 4): a young peasant woman, barefoot, pauses in her work of raking leaves; looking wistfully into the middle distance, she seems to wonder if there is not more to life than this?

In fields and factories
Nineteenth-century notes often carry pastoral scenes of women framed by fragrant floral bowers (fig. 41), or caressing sweet and friendly calves. Twentieth-century issues can be just as romantic, with graceful native girls balancing decorative baskets

40 *above left* Women preparing food without enthusiasm on a 200 cruzeiro note of Brazil, 1981. (153x73)
41 *above right* Maid churning butter on a 3 dollar note of the Bank of Ypsilanti, Michigan, 1837. (184x78)
42 *right* Women in dutiful feminine roles surround a tract on leading a good life,
on an unissued note from Shanghai, *c.*1880s. (113x178)

寅 邑
元增同記
認 不 票 認 人 留 心 仔 細 看 記
計㨗市錢
文

43 *above* Female worker in a textile factory on a 10 lek note of Albania, 1964. (135x75)

44 *left* Women working in paddy fields, with industry and transport in the background, on a 100 dong note of Vietnam, 1985. (157x78)

45 *below left* Young woman at a computer terminal on a 5000 dinar note from Macedonia (former Yugoslavia), 1992. (144x77)

46 *below right* A woman in national costume carries corn-ears and a scythe, traditional emblems of the cycle of life, death and rebirth. Detail from a 10 krooni note of Estonia, 1940. (148x94)

of produce on their heads or shoulders, but are often less poetic, bringing women in from the fields to the factory floor. As in the past, some notes carry themes related specifically to an important sector of a country's economy – cotton-picking in Mali, for instance (pl. 6). Others use more general images to represent agriculture and industry, as on a recent note of Vietnam depicting women working in paddy fields in the foreground, with factory chimneys in the distance (fig. 44). It is noticeable that 'hard' industrial images are seldom found on notes from western countries which, counting the costs and assuming the benefits of an industrial economy, tend to favour 'soft' subjects such as flora and fauna, history and heritage. For poorer nations, it can be a matter of pride to advertise industrial and technological development – witness the young woman at a computer terminal on the first notes of the newly independent state of Macedonia (fig. 45).

Unlike the domestic vignettes, there is little overt evidence of sexual stereotyping when women are shown at work; indeed men and women are often shown working together. Nonetheless, women on notes are rarely seen in what are conventionally regarded as male occupations, and whether they are continuing traditional labour patterns or are reflecting emancipation, they are not given positions of power. The implication is that women as a group do not have authority, which may instead be reserved for men, or an élite of either sex. Notes of communist China are a case in point: women are shown driving tractors and wearing trousers; they have been granted equality with men, but it is equality under oppression and despite the symbolism of their short, windswept hair, they have neither freedom nor power (pl. 8). The idealistic ideology of such imagery may, however, be double-edged, for although the superficial picture is one of justice and happiness, the propaganda is sufficiently blatant to reveal the underlying hypocrisy. The official line may therefore turn out to be unintentionally subversive.

State representatives

Superficially at least, those women who may be termed 'state representatives' seem to enjoy greater autonomy than those shown in domestic or working situations. Usually in national costume or surrounded by national emblems, they apparently have no function other than to give authority to the notes by embodying the country of issue. It is tempting to classify them as successors to Britannia and her like, their distinctive costumes replacing heraldic devices blazoned on the allegories' shields, but apart from their patriotic appearance, the two generations have little in common. One fundamental difference is that the modern women are not aggressive or war-like; they wear beautiful headdresses instead of helmets. This is to some degree a corollary of the more literal style of note design. As we have seen, money must carry images with positive associations, and while national identity has in practice often been preserved only by bitter fighting, military images on notes are relatively uncommon. When they do occur they are usually historical in context and almost always associated with men. By the same token, naturalistic portrayals of women

47 *above* Portrait of an Andalusian woman with a pot typical of the region, by the painter Julio Romero de Torres (1880-1930), on a 100 peseta note of the Bank of Spain, 1953. (137x88)
48 *below* Native woman with pots and flora and fauna on a 1000 franc note of French West Africa, 1952. Symbolically vases may suggest waters of life and fertility. (137x88)

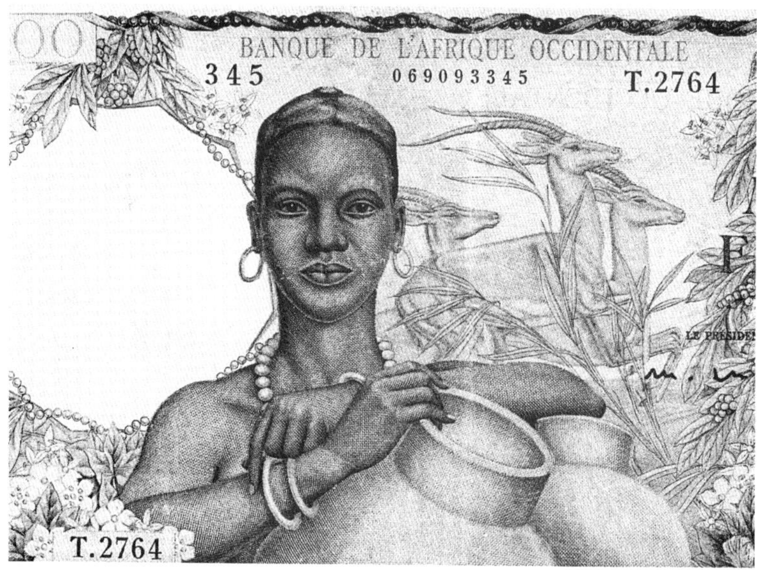

49 *right* Peasant woman harvesting roses for perfume on a 50 leva note of Bulgaria, 1951. (156x80)

must conform to the issuing authorities' view of society's expectations, and they therefore tend to have conventional feminine attributes. Traditional emblems of fruit, flowers, vegetables and grain still make a connection between women's fertility, agricultural output, and national prosperity. This timeless and universal symbolism also crosses geographical boundaries, as can be seen on two notes issued in Spain and West Africa in the early 1950s, each showing a woman resting her arms on a huge vase, and surrounded by lush, decorative vegetation (figs. 47,48).

Furthermore, despite their air of independence, the status of these national ambassadors is ambiguous. Certainly they are not engaged in menial work, but their very lack of employment combined with their glamorous appearance may give them the character of high-class cover-girls, and indeed, given the increasing power of central institutions responsible for note issue, it is possible that these images of women are chosen mainly to give their personality to the state, which can provide its own authority. Whatever abilities such women might have, they are used to serve, not to govern.

It is easy to read low status into the designs of colonial note issues showing cheerful natives enjoying the fruits of European rule. For modern observers these images can seem to be a form of exploitation, but they probably were not intended as such: however arrogant and patronising colonial administration may have been, at the time it was seen as benevolent paternalism, at least by those who practised it. Moreover, smiling indigenous peoples are just as frequently portrayed on the notes of countries after independence. It is interesting, however, to consider the images which represent the European power in allegorical form, and the colony as a realistic

50 *left* An unclothed native girl in the care of a fully draped western allegory,
on a 50 angolares note of Angola, 1947. (134x68). Angola was a Portuguese colony until 1975.
51 *right* A cheering crowd of several ethnic minorities extols the People's Republic of China.
Detail from a 5 yuan note of the People's Bank of China, 1953. (164x75)

52 *left* Nude female figure with cap of liberty, shield and eagle on a 5 dollar note
of the Commercial Bank of Columbus, Mississippi, 1846. (201x78)
53 *right* Allegorical women with exposed breasts and symbols of agriculture
on a 10 peso note of the Banco Oriental, Uruguay, 1867. (181x75)

figure, as in the Algerian note discussed above (Chap. 2), or the note of French West Africa. The fact that the indigenous peoples are shown as mere mortals does indeed emphasise their subject status, but it may be significant, too, that the mother country is personified by an allegorical female, implying either that women do not hold power, or if they do, that it must be disguised. Manipulative use of ethnicity to enhance the image of central government can also be seen on notes issued by the People's Bank of China. For example, a note of 1953 shows a group of ethnic minorities, apparently in Tiananmen Square, holding banners proclaiming 'long live the People's Republic of China' (fig. 51): issued only a few years after the proclamation of the Communist People's Republic in 1949, and the occupation of Tibet in 1950, the image is sheer political propaganda. Of course not all pictures of ethnic women need invite such cynicism; still there is a sense that this use of race, sometimes associated with gender, smacks of tokenism which undermines the real status of the peoples portrayed.

The body unadorned
In the early 1840s the chief clerk of the Austrian National Bank, Franz von Salzmann, proposed the adoption of nude figures on notes as protection against forgery, maintaining that they would make 'such a lasting impression even on any common man that he would immediately notice any deviation from the true likeness'. Von Salzmann was, however, careful to stipulate that the degree of nudity should be 'in keeping with decorum'.[15] This warning was sensible, not only to avoid offending the public, but because nakedness can symbolise base depravity as well as transcendent purity, and it is the latter image of incorruptibility that a bank or state treasury will want to convey. Bare-breasted liberty is one thing, a tousled libertine quite another, and, not surprisingly, there is little overt eroticism in nudity on banknotes. Few figures appear entirely naked, and those that do are either turning modestly away, or discreetly covering their hips with floral garlands or minimal folds of cloth. Most female nudes are shown naked from the waist upwards, exposing only their breasts, or often just one breast – imagery that is not necessarily sexual and may more readily be associated with motherhood and nourishment. And it is surely significant that semi-clad women on notes are found almost exclusively in the two contexts where they can reveal their bodies with modesty; that is, as classical allegory or native of a non-western country.

Symbolically, nudity is often associated with truth and the implication of openness and integrity was no doubt attractive for nineteenth-century private banks, some of which operated under rather dubious management. Defiant exposure as a symbol of liberty may also be a sign of authority, as for example on a local issue in Mississippi showing a nude female figure holding a cap of liberty and accompanied by an eagle perched on a shield (fig. 52). Recently, too, France has used a detail from Delacroix's painting of 'Liberty leading the People' alongside the artist's portrait, thus neatly combining cultural and political heritage (Chap. 2, fig. 22). A woman's breast is also

54 Brazen stares from allegories of fortune and agriculture on a 100 franc note of France, 1915. (186x111)

55 Softly draped Plenty with exposed breast and thigh, opposite a stony-faced labourer. (back of fig. 54)

56 Nudity symbolising purity and freedom on a 1000 mark note of Finland, 1922-45. (203x119)

a symbol of fertility, and often appears linked with agriculture, as with the two figures on a nineteenth-century note of Uruguay (fig. 53). These girls are particularly sweet, but then most allegorical nudes have a chaste demeanour. Indeed the most provocatively inviting glance comes from two fully clothed but raunchy creatures on a French note of 1915. The inadequately covered allegory on the back of the same note is much more demure, even though the positioning of her arms, in which she holds a cornucopia, gently emphasises her exposed breast and thighs, and the male labourer opposite her is firmly averting his gaze (figs. 54,55).

The spiritual significance of nudity is rarely used on naturalistic note designs, a distinctive exception being a series of Finnish notes introduced in 1922. A small community of men, women and children are shown naked but for a few notional draperies and decorously placed flower garlands. Walking through fertile countryside and lit from an unseen source, they represent humanity in a future paradise, and make no allusion to material wealth (fig. 56).

The semi-nakedness of women portrayed on non-western issues contains little ulterior symbolism because the women are shown in what is for them a normal state of dress. Their manner is unselfconscious, chaste and modest: indeed it is possible that the unaffected way in which they, and the allegories, reveal their bodies robs them of erotic power. Often these women are shown as mothers, or surrounded by plentiful fruits and vegetables to indicate their state's role as provider and sustainer of life. Nothing could be more wholesome, and yet there is an underlying ambiguity. The freedom symbolised by nudity can also suggest lack of control and the untamed force of nature as opposed to the civilising influence of culture. For those in societies

57 Woman as mother and source of life, shown in a family group on a 100 franc note
of French West Africa, 1948. (back of pl. 10; 162x90)

which associate nudity with privacy, the exposed bodies of women on non-western notes may arouse feelings of guilt at apparent exploitation and discomfiture at the challenge to our idea of civilisation. With tropical fruits, exotic costumes and glowing dusky skin, these beautiful women may stir up ideas of 'otherness', and the dangerous territory of instinct and intuition which is conventionally associated with the feminine principle. Nude images of women have perhaps the most multi-layered symbolism of all the female forms on paper money. They are, quite literally, the most explicit use of women's bodies as channels for imposed meaning, which officially shows woman's chastity and fertility as both representing and serving the state and society. At the same time, the self-contained serenity of these images gives them authority beyond their appointed role, for they remind us that by exercising individual choice in the way her body is used, a woman can exert considerable power.

58 Quiet authority in the figure of a native girl on a 500 franc note from the French colony of New Caledonia in the South Pacific, 1927-38. (218x150)

4 Beauty's Conquest
A woman's face

> *Let a florid music praise*
> *The flute and the trumpet*
> *Beauty's conquest of your face:*
> *In that land of flesh and bone*
> *Where from citadels on high*
> *Her imperial standards fly*
> *Let the hot sun*
> *Shine on, shine on.*
>
> W.H. Auden (1907-1973)

The face conquered by beauty is in turn empowered to attract, fascinate and command; so in the twentieth century, faces of women, real and imaginary, have brought charm and authority to paper currency. Images of human figures catch our attention, but we are drawn to faces in particular because they can reveal personality. Thus while allegorical and naturalistic figures of women have sometimes been given very realistic facial expressions, close-up images of faces alone are particularly appropriate for modern banknotes.

Early bankers with a limited track record and little legal backing chose note designs to emphasise their competence; nowadays central banks and state treasuries clearly have status, but they are remote and formal institutions which can well benefit from bringing a human touch to their public image. Indeed, a non-note-issuing Swiss commercial bank recently published an advertisement with a portrait of its founder, and the slogan 'A Private Bank with Personality'.[16]

However, the use of a historical portrait, accompanied by the date of the bank's foundation, is not in itself enough to guarantee success. Many banking failures have been caused by an excess of venal human nature over judicious management, and prudence and probity remain essential. As with the images already discussed, therefore, the faces of women on notes have a symbolic function, and must combine individual character with widely recognised good qualities. This applies even to portraits, for while notes may celebrate a particular woman's achievements, she in turn appears as a representative of her country.

The faces of women on paper money fall into two categories. Firstly, there are imaginary faces. These may share the attributes of classical allegories – Britannia's helmet or a cap of liberty, for example – or they may be naturalistic images of women who are contemporary and indigenous to the time and place of issue – these may be compared to the 'state representatives' of the previous chapter. Secondly, it has become commonplace for notes to carry a portrait of a major national figure, renowned for his or her achievement, and this can be seen as a variation on the scenes of women employed in domestic or professional work. In a few cases, portraits are shown three-quarter view or full-figure, but even in these cases, it is the face which attracts our attention. Generally speaking, idealised naturalistic faces of women began to appear on notes in the late nineteenth century, and have been replaced by portraits in the second half of the twentieth century. As with the other images, it would be wrong to impose too strict a pattern: there are portraits of monarchs on private British issues in the 1820s, and vignettes of Queen Victoria appeared on both local British notes and colonial issues. However, monarchs are perhaps a special case in that while the portraits on notes are certainly intended to be recognisable, they are there primarily in respect of their function as the ultimate embodiment of state authority. Personal character and facial expression are relatively unimportant and although they are portraits they can also be seen as a special set of the allegorical faces with their predominantly symbolic role. It is also true that some countries, especially in Africa, still use idealised heads, often with national headdresses, as cultural representatives. Nonetheless, there is a discernible move on twentieth-century notes away from idealised faces towards identifiable portraits.

In some respects this can be interpreted as a logical progression determined by several co-existing factors. One very practical consideration is the continuing need for greater security against forgery. The printing-plates for early notes were engraved entirely by hand; in the course of the nineteenth century, complex abstract designs produced by the geometric lathe (rose-engine) were introduced; and today, computer-generated graphics are employed. Despite the benefits of technology, however, it is still widely believed that fine hand-engraving is one of the hardest elements for the forger to copy, and faces provide exceptional scope for a good artist. Indeed, portrait engraving can become a specialisation within the already specialised field of banknote design. Although an idealised head may be highly distinctive, the portrait of a known person can be even more effective as a weapon against forgery. This is apparent with portraits of reigning monarchs whose faces are well known to the public; such familiarity is a daunting challenge even for the legitimate engraver and all the more so for one of unlawful intent, who must contend with the public's general awareness of a face and their recognition of its legitimate reproduction on notes.[17]

Two other influences which have encouraged the use of portraits are interrelated. One is the need for modern, impersonal note-issuers to bring personality to their product. Clearly there are constraints: faces dissolving into laughter or tears, however emotionally engaging, would not convey an appropriate sense of assurance and dignity; consequently most faces on notes, real or imaginary, share the same steady and serious gaze (fig. 59). But in spite of this similarity, the portraits, even of

59 *left* The cool appraising gaze of a classical Britannia on a 5 pound note
of the Bank of England, 1957. (158x89)
60 *right* Lady Lavery, wife of the artist Sir John Lavery, shown as Hibernia leaning on an Irish harp,
on a 10 pound note of the Central Bank of Ireland, 1951. (190x109)

women no longer living, tend to have a greater vitality – perhaps because the face
is already known, or because for both the engraver and the public, associations from
the person's life bring a certain humanity to their image. It is interesting, in this
respect, to consider the cases where artists have used real women as models for
allegorical heads – for example Lady Lavery as Hibernia on Irish notes from 1928 to
1976 (fig. 60).[18] She has a beautiful, memorable face, but we may wonder whether
women portrayed in this way are honoured by their elevation to national symbols,
or demeaned because they do not appear simply as themselves. Once again we are
reminded of the ambiguous nature of allegory, which both veils and reveals.

Portraits of famous women appearing in their own right lend something of their
character to the note and its issuing authority, thus counteracting the homogeneous
and anonymous nature of these centralised institutions. The emphasis on personality
as well as probity has grown with the changing status of banking and increased
regulation of note-issue, but the trend is not confined to that profession. It is
axiomatic now to say that advances in technology and communication have made

the world smaller; at the same time, economies of scale have led to business on an inhumanly large scale, and a loss of individuality and variety. Perhaps as an antidote to encroaching uniformity, the late twentieth century has also encouraged the right to personal choice, the value of personal achievement, and the admiration of individual heroes in many fields of endeavour, who thanks to mass-media can be celebrated and recognised across the world. With the exception of rulers and political figures, people portrayed on notes are seldom popular figures of stage or screen, but their prominence on national currencies is compatible with the modern cult of hero worship and encouragement of individual attainment.

High citadels

Idealised female faces on notes occupy an enchanted no-man's-land between allegory and realism, in that their lifelike faces are frequently embellished with symbolic accessories. Some have classical attributes appropriate for the political circumstances in which the note was issued: for example, Athena's helmet for a French note issued during World War I (pl. 13), or, still more significantly the turreted crown of Tyche, goddess of the city's fortune, on notes of Republican Spain (pl. 14).[19] Others carry more peaceful images of woman as giver and sustainer of life, as on two Austrian notes of the 1920s, one showing a woman with three small children, the other an elegant goddess of fertility holding a decoratively arranged cornucopia (figs. 61,62). Corn-ears are popular, too, perhaps as unusual hair ornaments, or sprouting amongst rococo swirls of acanthus designs.

Like the classical allegories, these women have a superhuman function, for they represent the spirit of a nation and the authority of the state. Often they are shown in profile, or looking coolly into the distance as if surveying their territory; when they do look at the viewer their gaze can be uncomfortably appraising, and sometimes literally superior, directed downwards from an elevated vantage point. At the same time, however, they have very human faces which can fix them in a certain time; thus the hairstyle of the girl on the French note above could only date to the 1910s, and makes her helmet disconcertingly similar to a cloche hat, while the clearly defined eyebrows and soft, wavy hair of the woman on a Bohemian note of 1940 are typical of her time (fig. 63). The specific and the universal are prettily combined in two glamorous women on a French colonial issue for Réunion dating to the 1940s: one with bright lips, scarf and tight curls is utterly contemporary, while the other wears a wreath of laurel, traditional symbol of victory and eternity (pl. 15).

As geographical indicators, female faces can be misleading, especially on nineteenth-century notes which tend to promote the picture of white, western supremacy. This may be explained in part by prevailing political and sociological ideology which still interpreted most cultures from an essentially European viewpoint, but it also illustrates what was then a common practice in note production of using standard 'off-the-peg' designs offered by engravers – thus the same beautiful profile of a very western girl with laurel in her long, loose hair can

61 *left* Plenty modelled by the note designer's mother, on a 50,000 kronen note of Austria, 1922. (193x105)
62 *right* Allegorical mother and children on a 500,000 kronen note of Austria, 1922. (199x106)

63 *left* The contemporary face of a woman on a 5 kronen note of Bohemia, 1940. (130x62)
64 *right* The lovely profile of a western allegory, seen here on a 500 mil reis note of Brazil, 1911. (191x87)

65 *left* A plumed helmet from western allegorical tradition worn by a Chinese woman,
on a 10 yuan note of the China and South Sea Bank Ltd, 1927. (179x89)
66 *centre and right* Women with traditional Chinese costume and almond-shaped faces. (back of fig. 65)

67 *left* Women wearing native jewellery and headdresses on a 100 franc note of French West Africa, 1936. (164x95)
68 *right* HM Queen Elizabeth II, the first monarch portrayed on Bank of England notes,
as she appeared on the 1 pound note of 1960-78. (150x71)

be found on notes issued in Canada and Brazil, both printed by the American Bank Note Company (fig. 64). One of the most curious examples of misplaced culture is the classically allegorical plumed helmet worn by a distinctly Oriental woman on a note of the China and South Sea Bank (fig. 65). This intrusive symbol of authority is, however, balanced by the heads of women wearing the headdresses of regional ethnic minorities, some of whom have the almond-shaped faces traditionally regarded in China as a sign of beauty (fig. 66). As with images of women's bodies, it is indeed non-European countries which are most likely to give faces a distinct national identity. This is often evident on notes from Africa and islands of the Pacific and Indian oceans, which both as colonies and independent states tend to show women with dramatic national or ceremonial headdresses.

Idealised faces of women are among the loveliest images on notes, which in combining allegory and realism can create a striking symbolism. Their solemn beauty gives them an air of timeless authority, but their believable faces suggest that real women might aspire to the power hitherto embodied by allegories.

Imperial standards

Female heads of state depicted on notes are a select group which can justifiably claim to belong with both idealised faces and portraits, for although they are images of real women, they appear not for their personal qualities, but as representatives of the authority invested in their office. As with other portraits, those of female rulers are predominantly a feature of the second half of the twentieth century; indeed, Bank of England notes did not carry a portrait of the reigning monarch until 1960 (fig. 68). To some extent, therefore, the portrayal of heads of state is compatible with the modern cult of the individual. Nowadays too, portraits of living monarchs have a practical benefit for paper money in that public familiarity with the person's face is an additional challenge to forgers. In *The Trumpet Major*, Thomas Hardy describes how the heroine, Anne, recognises George III in his carriage 'by seeing a profile reminding her of the current coin of the realm';[20] in Britain today it is because we know the face of the Queen so well from newspaper photographs and television that we recognise her at once on banknotes. Alan Dow, who has engraved many portraits of the Queen for British and Commonwealth issues, has pointed out that he can never capture a perfect likeness, as everyone has their own idea of the Queen's face;[21] however, once a portrait on a note is well-established it will join the other mass-media as a source of our knowledge: witness the complaints in Britain about the introduction of an older image of the Queen on the new £5 note introduced in 1990, even though it simply reflected the inescapable fact of ageing. The public's critical faculty is however an equal problem for counterfeiters, who would be rash to attempt engraving a portrait. For an accurate copy they must rely on photo-mechanical means of reproduction, but this will not produce the raised texture of intaglio printing on authentic notes, created by printing from an engraved plate.

69 The imperial splendour of Catharine II of Russia (1762-96), protected by a semi-clad male warrior, on a 100 rouble note of Russia, 1910-17. (259x121)

In fact, relatively few of the small number of female heads of state pictured on notes are contemporary rulers. Most like portraits generally on notes, are of past leaders. Indeed part of their appeal may lie in the recognition history has granted to their achievements as leaders of their country – this could apply, say, to Catharine the Great under whose rule the Russian empire was greatly expanded (fig. 69). It is interesting too that even countries which no longer have monarchies may illustrate past monarchs on their notes, suggesting that their historical status together with the tradition and power of royalty has become appropriate symbolism of state authority. Portraits of historical leaders may therefore be effective images for two rather contradictory reasons. On the one hand, because they are real people, their faces generally have more character and personal impact than imaginary allegories; on the other, living people whom we know even indirectly, may be almost too real, because they are seen to be human and therefore fallible, while portraits of historical rulers can offer a combination of real personality with legendary authority.

70 *left* Head of Nefertiti, queen of Egypt, 14th century BC, on a 5 piastre note of Egypt, 1940. (95x58)
71 *right* Zenobia, warrior-queen of Palmyra, 3rd century BC, on a 100 pound note of Syria, 1990. (166x80)

72 *left* Engraving of Queen Victoria on a 5 dollar note of St. Stephen's Bank, Canada, 1860. (188x77)
73 *right* Queen Victoria on a 1 pound note for the Bank of Victoria, Australia, *c*.1860. (194x115)

Of these two elements, it is the second, symbolic role which is more important. Images of women from ancient and classical history, such as Nefertiti in Egypt (fig. 70), or Zenobia of Palmyra in Syria (fig. 71) are not likenesses of photographic accuracy, but romantic impressions of women whose power and beauty are now almost mythical. It is just as true, however, of portraits of living rulers who are there as embodiments of the state. This is perhaps not obvious with regard to our current Queen, whose features are so familiar, but may be more easily seen in contemporary nineteenth-century vignettes of Queen Victoria, shown in imperial splendour on notes across the globe from Canada to Australia (figs. 72,73). In style and symbolic significance she effectively replaces figures of Britannia used a few years earlier, thus pointing up their shared purpose on notes as allegories of authority.

Flesh and bone

Portraits of women other than heads of state form an exceptional group amongst female images on paper money, in that they have earned their place through the personal achievements of the women portrayed. They are predominantly a feature which began in the later twentieth century, and they owe their popularity to several contemporary concerns, including the security offered by fine portraits, the general value placed on individual endeavour, and, sometimes, a deliberate effort to acknowledge officially (or at least not to ignore) the wide-ranging achievements of women. These portraits, above all others, show the human face of banking; they are the least formal and most personable – indeed, in many instances the women are shown smiling. Because the subjects are almost invariably historical figures, it is usually their names and reputations that are well known, not their physical features. The security value of the images therefore lies not in recognition of a particular face, but in the technical skill of the engraver and the power of human faces to attract our attention. Banknote designers and engravers often spend months researching and creating one portrait in an attempt to capture the character of the individual.

74 *left* Maria Montessori (1870-1952), the Italian doctor who developed the Montessori Method
of education, on a 1000 lira note of Italy, 1990. (111x61)
75 *centre* Golda Meir, prime minister of Israel from 1969 to 1974, on a 10 new sheqalim note
of the Bank of Israel, 1985. (137x76)
76 *right* The artist Angelika Kauffmann (1741-1807) on a 100 schilling note of Austria, 1969. (150x75)

In addition to meeting modern demands for individuality, portraits of women must also comply with the perennial requirement for note designs to convey positive qualities relating to national identity and integrity. In this sense, the achievements of the women portrayed are now placed at the service of the state and their individual lives take on a wider symbolic role. This will obviously have a bearing on which women are considered suitable for notes, and there is clearly a strong argument in favour of historical figures, whose status is already established, so that they have become part of a country's heritage. In this respect portraits of national heroes, male or female, conform to a popular trend on notes of industrialised countries to define a clear national identity in terms of their glorious past, although many of the people chosen have received recognition on an international scale. The women depicted do not form a homogeneous group; they include artists and poets, social campaigners and political activists. Furthermore they are not linked by any common, inherent 'female' characteristic, which places them in marked contrast to those allegorical and naturalistic idealisations which refer to the biological function of woman. Indeed most of the real women shown on notes are celebrated for attainments which have also been associated with men, and many have exhibited quite 'masculine' traits of initiative and leadership. This applies even to women in traditionally female occupations: Florence Nightingale is not honoured just because she was a gentle and devoted nurse, but because of her courage and determination in revolutionising the appalling conditions in the barrack hospital at Scutari during the Crimean War, and for her contribution to the teaching of nursing in Britain.[22]

Because of their dual status as individuals and national symbols, portraits of real women on notes send out ambivalent messages. Firstly, there is the paradox that women who may have been regarded as controversial during their lives have with time become establishment figures, and it is a moot point whether appearing on official state-controlled currency invokes their pioneering spirit or relegates it to the safe realms of history. Secondly, and more fundamentally, there is a sense in which raising the profile of individual achievement lessens the impact of a wider female symbolism. Some may feel that this is to be welcomed, in that specifically female symbolism is in itself discriminatory and demeaning, while others will argue that just because many images of women on banknotes have conformed to stereotyped perceptions does not mean that they all do, or need to. Portraits of women on recent note issues certainly break out from the confines of traditional female roles, and acknowledge the wide arena of activities in which women have excelled. But this very excellence is the problem, for few people can demonstrate the outstanding courage, intellect or ability of the women whose lives are commemorated on currency. For all their ambiguity, many female allegories are endowed with character and strength, and precisely because they are allegorical and allusive, they can provide a universal image of female authority to which any woman may aspire.

5 What is Beauty Anyway?
The message of women on notes

What is beauty, anyway?
                                    Pablo Picasso (1881-1973)

For two hundred years, paper money across the world has been adorned by images of women. They have appeared as armed warriors, tender nymphs, caring mothers, enticing charmers, hard-working peasants, national heroines – and sometimes just as beautiful women. Amongst this variety, it is nevertheless possible to discern patterns. These diverse and diverting creatures have been summoned for a common purpose: to impart a sense of viability and value to the notes on which they appear, and to the bank or country which issues them. This constant factor has led to several themes recurring across boundaries of time and place, but different societies have also introduced variations appropriate to their cultures and the changing circum-stances of note issue. Images of women on banknotes therefore convey a two-fold message: at one level they present an official text confirming the status of the currency; at another they reveal aspects of prevailing attitudes and beliefs in the societies which created them.

In this regard it is interesting, and more than a little ironic, that female images have often been used to represent power and authority on banknotes in societies where women have had little control over money in either domestic or professional situations. Indeed banking is traditionally viewed as a male profession, and even today, senior managers in banks and treasuries are generally men,[23] as are most banknote designers and engravers: virtually all images of women on paper money have therefore been chosen, designed and drawn by men. This does not, of course, invalidate the images, but the perspective from which they are drawn will inevitably have some impact on their meaning.

The powerful nature of allegorical female figures on nineteenth-century notes may seem surprising for a time when women had little legal control in matters of finance or property. However, as we have seen, many of these figures are ambiguous, female but not feminine, and often barricaded in masculine armour. Above all, they are imaginary. There is ambivalence too in the luscious portrayals of allegorical and naturalistic women who represent agriculture and plenty. Here the association of wealth with fertility goes to the heart of woman's biological role, which is potentially a fundamental source of power. Yet it can be argued that even this power is limited

77 *top* A classically beautiful profile on a 5 dollar note of the Sterling Bank of Canada, 1914. (191x83)

78 *left* Woman playing a traditional instrument on a Japanese clan-note from Hita, 1865. (45x158)
79 *right* The Statue of Liberty represents western influences on a 1 dollar note
of the Chinese-American Bank of Commerce, Shanghai, 1920. (142x72)

80 Fruits of plenty on a 5 pound note of the Provincial and Suburban Bank, Melbourne, 1896. (198x116)

when it is harnessed to the growth of a male-dominated society, and indeed goddesses of Plenty on notes yield their ripe crops in the service of the state economy. It is paradoxical that while the fluid, changeable aspects of women's bodies can be perceived by men as alien and alarming, nonetheless female forms are often chosen to represent great and constant virtues. The explanation may lie in the ambiguous and fanciful nature of the images, which, in personifying abstract qualities, depersonalise the women, thus allowing them to be safely accommodated in a male culture.

Perhaps the clearest pattern in the portrayal of women on banknotes is the chronological progression from classical allegories to portraits. Superficially it is tempting to see this as a shift from a notional power to a demonstration of real female authority, but at each stage of change the meaning of the images is ambiguous and open to different interpretations. From one viewpoint the allegories may appear to personify power in fantasy female figures; from another they may seem at least to acknowledge the idea, however masked, of women having authority. During the twentieth century, classical allegories have largely given way to realistic scenes of women in domestic occupations, in local communities, and at work, but despite the realism the images remain symbolic, and it is noticeable that most of the women are engaged in traditional domestic tasks or low-status work. More recently, portraits of real people have become a common element of banknote

81 Women representing an educated, literate society on a 20 shilling note of Kenya, 1986. (145x76)

design. In addition to heads of state, these increasingly include individuals celebrated for their achievements in the arts, science, politics and human welfare, and in the last ten years or so, many countries have made a deliberate decision to depict women. Such recognition of women's achievements will be appreciated by most people as part of the move towards sexual equality, yet it may also be said that because of their exceptional lives, these women indirectly highlight the more mundane lives of most of their sex. Appropriately enough, several of the women portrayed on notes were committed campaigners for the poor and underprivileged, a class which many would say includes women.

The shift from allegory to portrait involves a curious interaction between symbols and reality, for though the images become more lifelike, reflecting the growing visibility and power of women in modern society, their function remains symbolic. Allegories bestowed their admirable qualities on the money they adorned, but there is an impression that the realistic images and portraits of women are used not so much for their own personal qualities as to represent the beneficence of the state, and that those whose portraits appear are somehow honoured by being chosen to grace the national currency. This change has occurred as the right to issue notes has become increasingly centralised and official. While it is generally true that paper money reflects the society in which it circulates, it may more accurately be said of modern notes that they carry a view of society which the authorities wish to project. Once again, this does not necessarily mean that the images are bad or inaccurate, simply that they are likely to be partial.

Though a study of images of women on paper money is sharply focused, it raises wider questions regarding the impact of designs on currency – which is a kind of state advertising – and the portrayal of women in a medium used by millions and taken for granted. Indeed, although people may not be able to name the celebrities illustrated on the different denominations of notes of their own country, in practice they can quickly distinguish between them, and so must recognise the designs subliminally. Any interpretation of these images will, naturally enough, be affected by the viewer's own preconceptions; for example, the tempting charge of exploitation against nudity in pictures of native women on colonial notes may simply be the late-twentieth-century view of political correctness imposed on another society with different values. It is also true that even deliberate propaganda may not have the intended effect, as with the rose-tinted view of female tractor-drivers in China. The point is that these images matter because they are reproduced on objects which are mass-produced for public consumption. The very status of banknotes seems to give official sanction to the images they carry, which thus perpetuate our overt and latent perceptions of women. Beauty may be in the eye of the beholder, but it is far from being merely skin-deep. Those who issue and design money cannot avoid the practical constraints imposed by the nature of the product, nor can they escape the influences of heritage and culture. But while the millions of us who use banknotes are to some extent a captive audience, we do not have to be gullible: we can choose to look, and question what we see.

82 A woman's work is never done ... a weary allegory
rests from her labours on a 50 peso note
of the Banco Oriental, Uruguay, 1867. (197x86)

References

1   Letter to the Society of Arts, published in the *Report of the Committee of the Society of Arts ... relative to the mode of preventing the Forgery of Bank Notes*, London, 1819, p.43.

2   Ibid.

3   *An Inquiry into the Nature and Causes of the Wealth of Nations*, 1776, Chapter II, Book II, Chicago, 1976, p.310. Adam Smith (1723-90) was a Scottish philosopher and economist; his *Wealth of Nations* is celebrated as one of the earliest and greatest works on political economy.

4   An exception is the development of machine-produced abstract patterns for security printing.

5   For an absorbing account of female images as metaphor, see Marina Warner's excellent *Monuments and Maidens. The Allegory of the Female Form*, Pan, London, 1987. M. Esther Harding's *Woman's Mysteries*, Random Century, London, 1991, explores the role of the feminine principle in myth, story and dream.

6   *Morning Chronicle*, 20 December 1825, quoted in L.S. Pressnell, *Country Banking in the Industrial Revolution*, Oxford, 1956, pp.487-8.

7   I am grateful to Michael O'Hanlon for this information. The Wahgi people's attitudes to money and exchange are discussed in his book *Paradise: Portraying the New Guinea Highlands*, London, 1993.

8   See, for example, M. Esther Harding, op. cit., pp.49-50, on ancient associations of the moon goddess with animals.

9   Such associations are not only made in western folklore; thus in east Nigeria in the early 19th century, women were known as 'the trees which bear fruit' (Caroline Ifeka-Moller, 'Female Militancy and Colonial Revolt', in *Perceiving Women*, S. Ardener, ed., London, 1975, p.136).

10 See M. Warner, op. cit., p.124.

11 See M. Warner, op. cit., pp.124-5, on the patriarchal significance of female figures in armour, and *Images of Women in Peace and War. Cross-Cultural and Historical Perspectives*, Sharon Macdonald, Pat Holden and Shirley Ardener, eds., Basingstoke, 1987, p.7, on the Amazons and Boadicea as exceptions proving the power of male rule.

12 Jaap Bolten, *Dutch Banknote Design. A Compendium*, Amsterdam, 1988, p.35. The romantically-drawn connection between labour and prosperity was seen as outdated and patronising.

13 The geometric logos adopted by some banks are a case in point; on the other hand, the symbolic human figures used currently in the advertising for, say, British Telecom and Mercury Communications may signal a return to more personal corporate images.

14 Entitled 'Patria', the painting is by the Brazilian artist Pedro Bruno (1888-1949).

15 Quoted in W. Kranister, *The Moneymakers International*, Cambridge, 1989, p.111.

16 The advertisement for E. Gutzwiller et Cie, bankers in Basel and Geneva, appeared in Sotheby's Sales Diary for Autumn 1993, and carried a portrait of Carl Gutzwiller (1856-1928).

17 Portraits are also often used for the watermarks on banknotes, often depicting the same person whose face is reproduced in the note design.

18 Wife of the Irish painter, Sir John Lavery (1856-1941). The engraving on the notes is by John Harrison, based on a portrait by Lavery. See Derek Young, *Guide to the currency of Ireland. Legal tender notes 1928-1972*, Dublin, 1972, p.8.

19 That is, a crown symbolising the city walls, rather than a monarch's crown.

20 Thomas Hardy, *The Trumpet Major*, Pan Books Ltd., 1987 edition, p.95.

21 Mike Hutchins, 'Profile of a Portrait Engraver' in *Penrose 1982, International Review of the graphic arts*, London, 1981, pp.8-28.

22 A portrait of Florence Nightingale, against a background view of the Scutari hospital, appeared on the back of the Bank of England 10 pound note issued between 1975 and 1992.

23 The first woman was appointed to the Court of Directors of The Bank of England on 1st March 1993.

Index